APOSTASY

APOSTASY

John Burnside

DARE-GALE PRESS

First published in Great Britain by Dare-Gale Press, 2022

2 3 4 5 6 27 26 25 24

www.daregale.com

Distributed by Central Books.

ISBN 9780993331190

Thanks are due to *London Review of Books* in which two of these poems first appeared.

Front cover image: Joseph Mallord Turner, 'Channel Sketchbook' page 55, Yale Center for British Art, Paul Mellon Collection.

Font: Typeset in 10/11pt Delicato, designed by Stefan Hattenbach.

Printed in England by One Digital Brighton on GF Smith paper certified by both Cradle to Cradle and the Forest Stewardship Council. Dare-Gale Press is committed to environmentally conscious publishing.

i.m. Adam Zagajewski

Jesus saw Nathanael coming to him, and saith of him, Behold an Israelite indeed, in whom is no guile! Nathanael saith unto him, Whence knowest thou me?

John I 47-48

L'homme doit chercher son état à venir dans le présent, et le ciel, non point au-dessus de la terre, mais en soi.

Ignaz-Vitalis Troxler

I A Footnote to Colossians

For ye are dead, and your life is hid
St Paul

Let us remember
the stillborn: how they

cede their places here
with such good grace

that no one ever
speaks of them

again.
In school,

we placed them, carefully,
in Limbo,

deep in the folds of smoke
and snowfall, where

their names would never
find them:

pagan, now,
and immaterial,

like phantoms,
or that

boy I sometimes saw
in polaroids,

the one they said
was me.

II Nativity

A spill of yew
like Christ's blood
in the snow;
and somewhere in the hedge,
just yards away,
a fleck of presence
waiting to be born.

No angel at the gate.
No guiding star.
We make this world
from gravity and light
and we alone, God's grace
by other means:

a flock of redwings
flitting through the fog,
woodrush
and fescue,
wintergreen,
Rose of Sharon.

III Midnight Mass

We brought the starlight in
fresh from the cold,

a rumour on the skin
of some old

fiefdom, pagan, kindred to the other
animals — *the boarhound and the boar*,

the gaunt deer on the roads
like refugees.

Convinced of nothing,
least of all the saints,

I spent my last prayer
on a plaster

Virgin, paintwork
flaking on an upraised

finger, seams
of gypsum

in the creases
of her veil,

but nothing came to pass,
beyond the scent

of spruce and tallow,
menthol, *L'air du temps,*

and later, when we walked home
after Mass,

I asked the sky for nothing
save the blue

of daybreak, first sun,
magpies in the snow.

IV Verses for a Sampler

Rain at the gates
and the ghost of a mother is here.
Pink-lipped with the blush
of Candlemas, and plainly
fabled, she is older than the girl
who raised us, less
impersonal, though
not above suspicion.

Nightly we lay her down
in her bed of needles,
patient as mice, enthralled
by the thought
of Forever;
nightly we wait in vain
for the *Ecce Virgo*,

a local hajj, the spell
of alpenglow,
a phantom horseman
from some Medieval
woodcut, *Homo*
ludens, with a taste for calculus.

Thou knowest, Lord,
the secrets of our hearts:
a sea-wind blowing in
from street to street.

A final orchard.

Blossom in the ruins.

V Out-take from The Gospel of Narcissus

Another skin has come
to nothing, like the snow that fell all day

and melted
in the space between the trees.

Another shadow, cousin to the one
I wanted, when I came in from the cold,

an Old Believer, skilled
in saddle-stitch

and lorinery, my elders
gathered round the bonfire with their dogs

and shotguns, patient, ready to begin,
and every man alone beneath the stars.

VI Sketch for a Stabat Mater

Two, two, the lily-white boys,
Clothed all in green

As if there was a Queen, or miles
of starlight in the backroom where I played
the shadow of a lily-white
in aspic,

I kept faith with the gravity
of objects
and waited for the carriage to arrive
that someone from the past would surely send

to fetch me, horses
lifelike in the dark,
the murmur in the hall that might have been
a spring rain, or a dawning, all I knew

from Old Moore and The Joyful Mysteries
come good at last, as if my heart was true.

VII The Heresy of the Free Spirit

Visible only in rain, or the blue of daybreak,
more of a thought than a form I could have named,
heaven was void
and the angels were always too bright
to be observed.

No God to speak of, there, beyond the glide
of something at the far end of the yard
that never came to pass,
though it was true:

a hunger, pure and simple, like the nub
of pulse and slime
that would have made a soul
had I been born with nothing to repent,
and nothing to forgive, save grace and favour.

VIII Concerning guile

Because I have mislaid the hush
of boyhood — snowfalls;

shadows in the trees —
too often I have been

indelicate.

And yet, beyond the provinces
of guile, there is

an *autremonde* more
Tir na Nog than

not:
      though not
the refuge I had wished for,

being lost.

If this skin shows too much, let it be
flayed: not

sweetly, but with no great
drama, ice

or laser in the lull
of witching-hour.

No afterlife to come, nor any
persons who aspire

to martyry, dismantled as they are
by Being

Beauteous
    which is no life at all.

IX Sweet Jams and Spikenard

Luke 18: 34

A skinned child
in the field, just raw enough
to be immaculate,
I hoped I would not fall
to wedlock,
or the snare
of Mother Church.

No summers, then,
that I remember now,
no afterburn
of neon on my tongue,
only the grace
to nurse a false amen
through parlour games
and Quinquagesima.

That Covenant
is lost, Gethsemane
gone down to dust
and buried in the stone,
and nothing in this house
that I can use,
no alibi for love, no *comme il faut*,
no motion in the heart
that is not blood.

X Auto-da-fé

Unshriven, and impervious to doubt,
he's out there, with his doppelgänger smile,

shining a light through the Tree
of Knowledge, almost

saintly in his armature
of fire.

One of the chosen, practised in the art
of touch-me-not, he constantly arrives

at weightlessness, a wick of skin and bone
too lifelike to be true;
                    and yet he goes

unquenched, a beacon
blazing in the sun,

my sinless other, bending
to the flame,

so pure and bright,
he almost pulls me in.

XI Ash Wednesday

Abandon was its own
safe haven, one more incidence
of comfort, cindered palms
and chrism in the likeness
of a cross
— *pulvis es, et in pulverem reverteris* —

a loose stitch in the heart
made visible: my mind
a flashlight ghosting the walls
at change of shift,
my body hand-me-down
and fictive, almost
Lenten, cleansed
and whittled: nerveless, hollow to the bone

— *et mittere digneris sanctum Angelum tuum de caelis,*
qui benedicat, et sanctificet hos cineras —

XII Litha

In summer, it was harder to be churched;
the pagan gods were out, their sentries
drifting through the sunlit

chapel, pollen
scattered on the flagstones like some timeless
scripture from a world before the Word.

Set loose from school,
I wandered with the bees
through Willowherb and Himalayan

Balsam
          catching
shadows in the shadows: inklings, figments of the land's
imagining;

and nothing to reveal, beyond the hum
of incarnation:
sun on the backlot, mayweed, that lingering smell

of bird rot in the grass, like
angel spoor. How sweetness is always
ruin. No

Hereafter. Always now.

XIII A Note on the Sethian Heresy

For lust of knowing what should not be known,
we take the Golden Road to Samarkand.
James Elroy Flecker

A shred of Samarkand, but not
begotten, like the navy-drab
of worship.
No more
chapel, no more
sinner at the gate,

though shadows pass, gigantic on the sand,
and softly through the silence
beat the bells.

I thought it might approximate
to home, so very

picturesque
and measured,

like a service
of remembrance:
fragments of *très riches heures,*
scenes from a masque,
a stronghold sure
against the days
of ruin.

XIV Apostasy

Psalms 139: 23

At one time,
when there might have been a God,
the side-streets vaguely
convent, gospel
whispered down the galleries
of rain,

I would have been awake for almost
nothing in the perishable world,
the Presence half-revealed, improbable,
lighting the hedge like a flame
in the green
of morning.

No convent now.
Only the sway of matter and a hint
of distance, almost
perfect, like a favourable *feng shui,*
or like the sudden lull that comes
late in the afternoon,
when an angel passes:

sunlight dusting the pines
by the harbour wall
and nobody saying a word
till day is done,
pilgrim again, beyond all destination,
white in the light of the moon, white in the dawn,
white in the daylight
and haunted by nothing at all.